THE GREAT LITTLE BOOK OF SALADS

dress it up

THE GREAT LITTLE BOOK OF SALADS

dress it up

Emma Summer

southwater

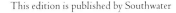

This edition is published by Southwater

Distributed in the UK by
The Manning Partnership
251–253 London Road East
Batheaston
Bath BA1 7RL
tel. 01225 852 727
fax 01225 852 852

Distributed in Canada by
General Publishing
895 Don Mills Road
400–402 Park Centre
Toronto, Ontario M3C 1W3
tel. 416 445 3333
fax 416 445 5991

Distributed in Australia by
Sandstone Publishing
Unit 1, 360 Norton Street
Leichhardt
New South Wales 2040
tel. 02 9560 7888
fax 02 9560 7488

Southwater is an imprint of Anness Publishing Limited
Hermes House, 88–89 Blackfriars Road, London SE1 8HA
tel. 020 7401 2077; fax 020 7633 9499

© Anness Publishing Limited 1996, 2004
Printed in China

Publisher Joanna Lorenz
Senior Cookery Editor Linda Fraser
Assistant Editor Emma Brown
Designers Patrick McLeavey & Jo Brewer
Illustrator Anna Koska
Photographers Karl Adamson, Michael Michaels, James Duncan,
Steve Baxter, Amanda Heywood & Edward Allwright
Recipes Christine France, Roz Denny, Catherine Atkinson, Hilaire Walden,
Steven Wheeler, Annie Nichols, Shirley Gill & Norma MacMillan

Previously published as *The Little Salad Cookbook*

1 3 5 7 9 10 8 6 4 2

NOTES

Standard spoon and cup measures are level.

Large eggs are used unless otherwise stated.

Contents

Introduction

Thanks to the abundance of good quality salad-stuffs in our supermarkets, these once seasonal treats can now be enjoyed every day. It is true that there's a special pleasure in gathering greens and fresh herbs from the garden, but when summer gives way to autumn, and even the cut-and-come again lettuces no longer yield fresh young leaves, it is satisfying to know that salads can still be on the menu.

There's no better way to exercise artistic flair than in assembling a salad. Even a simple green salad can offer subtle variations in shape, texture, colour and flavour. Contrast a crisp iceberg lettuce with a soft butterhead; the pale leaves of lollo biondo with the matt glossy green of watercress. Balance bland flavours with a few leaves of bitter escarole, or introduce an underlying lemon flavour with some shreds of sorrel. Nasturtium leaves add a peppery tang, as does rocket, while young spinach leaves are valued for their rich sweetness. For extra colour, choose the red or purple hues of oakleaf, lollo rosso or red cabbage, perhaps accentuated by a few feathery leaves from the heart of a frisée lettuce. Take care not to overdo it; two or three different types of leaf, chosen for their complementary or contrasting qualities, will be more effective than an ill-assorted medley.

As for extra ingredients, the list is almost endless. Salad vegetables include avocados, artichokes, asparagus, green beans, carrots, cauliflower florets, celery, cucumber, fennel, peppers of every colour, radishes and onions, especially Spanish or mild red onions. Tomatoes too, although these are often served on their own, with a simple olive oil dressing and snippings of basil. Vinegar is seldom added because tomatoes are themselves acidic. Fruits, especially oranges, apples, pears, grapes and melons, frequently feature in salads.

Potato salads are in a category of their own, and there are also many hearty salads based on rice, pasta or grains, including the famous tabbouleh. Meats, fish and shellfish make a major contribution.

In a formal meal, it is traditional to serve a simple salad after the entrée, to cleanse the palate before dessert, but a salad can serve equally well as a starter, accompaniment or substantial main course.

Salads were originally seasoned solely with salt (hence the name) but are now inseparably associated with a whole host of dressings, from simple mixtures of oil and vinegar or lemon juice to sauces based on mayonnaise, yogurt or blue cheese. Hot dressings, often with a foundation of bacon fat (the crisp fried bacon giving the salad extra flavour and texture) are increasingly popular, but must be added only at the last minute; if either dinner or diner is late, the leaves will become limp and the salad will be spoiled.

We are constantly being encouraged to eat more fresh vegetables and fruit. What better way to enjoy these ingredients than in a salad that is as pleasing to look at and to make as it is delicious to eat?

Familiar Salad Leaves

BUTTERHEAD LETTUCE

Also known as cabbage lettuce, because of its shape, this has soft leaves with a slightly buttery taste.

CHINESE LEAF

Two types of this crunchy vegetable are commonly seen; one is longer and more pointed than the other. Both have delicately flavoured long, crinkly leaves with crisp, white stems. It is available all year round and keeps well in the fridge.

COS LETTUCE

Firm, tapering leaves with a stiff central rib, tightly packed to form an elongated head, the cos or romaine lettuce is one of the most familiar and most widely available salad vegetables.

ENDIVE

There are several varieties of this loose-leaved salad vegetable: Batavian endive (escarole) has broad, ragged leaves, while the leaves of curly endive (frisée) are frilly, almost spiky. A red broad-leafed variety, radicchio, is favoured for its colour and texture. All endives tend to be rather bitter.

ICEBERG LETTUCE

With its large, firm head and tightly packed, crisp leaves, this is one of the most popular varieties of lettuce. It keeps for longer than most lettuces.

LAMB'S LETTUCE

Also known as corn salad or mâche, lamb's lettuce consists of small smooth green leaves in clusters. The leaves have a mild, sweet flavour. It is preferable to buy lamb's lettuce loose in whole plants, since it is fragile and bruises easily.

LITTLE GEM

Resembling a miniature cos lettuce, the Little Gem has neat well-formed oval leaves with a slightly nutty flavour.

LOLLO BIONDO/LOLLO ROSSO

Mild-tasting lollo lettuces have distinctive, frilly leaves forming a loose head. Lollo biondo is pale and creamy; rosso has leaves tinged with dark red.

OAKLEAF LETTUCE

Also known as feuille de chêne and red salad bowl, this lettuce is favoured for its colour (bronze to purple) and its delicate flavour. It has loose leaves branching from a single stalk.

ROCKET

This easy-to-grow, old-fashioned salad herb rewards gardeners with irregular, small, dark leaves which have a peppery flavour with a hint of citrus.

SALAD CRESS

Cress is bought growing in small trays or boxes; one simply snips off what is needed. It is a popular and pretty salad ingredient.

SORREL

The soft, spade-shaped leaves of this herb have a delicate lemony taste. Use raw sorrel sparingly. It does not keep well and must be bought very fresh.

SPINACH

Tender young spinach leaves have a sweet flavour and are delicious with bacon.

WATERCRESS

Watercress leaves are dark and glossy and grow on sprigged stems. Watercress is a member of the mustard family, as one might suppose from its peppery flavour.

Techniques

CHOOSING SALAD LEAVES

For the best flavour and texture, salad leaves must be fresh. Reject any that are wilted or discoloured. Buy or pick only what you can use within the next day or two, and store them in the fridge.

PREPARING SALAD LEAVES

To prepare lettuces, remove the coarse outer leaves, separate the remaining leaves and wash them well. Take care to remove any grit, but do not leave them to soak. Drain well, break off any tough ribs and dry the leaves. Use a salad spinner for the more robust leaves; blot delicate leaves with kitchen paper or a clean absorbent towel. If you must prepare lettuces ahead of time, pack the leaves into polythene bags, close tightly and store in the fridge.

MAKING A SIMPLE DRESSING

Dressings should be carefully chosen in order to complement the ingredients, and should not dominate the salad. A wide range of recipes appears in this collection, but for a simple French dressing the rule of thumb is to use three parts of olive oil to one part of wine vinegar, adding a pinch each of caster sugar, salt and pepper, and mustard powder or made mustard, for flavouring. Either combine all the ingredients in a screw-top jar, close tightly and shake well, or mix together the vinegar and the flavourings, then whisk in the oil.

TOSSING A GREEN SALAD

Rub the inside of the salad bowl with a cut clove of garlic, if you like. Just before serving, toss the leaves with just enough dressing to coat them. It is better to err on the mean side than to swamp the salad.

TOPPINGS

• Crumbled crisp bacon or toasted nori (dried seaweed)
• Toasted sunflower, sesame or pumpkin seeds
• Snipped chives, chopped parsley or other fresh herbs
• Grated hard-boiled egg (white and yolk)
• Grated cheese
• Slivers of sun-dried tomato
• Cubes of feta cheese or smoked tofu

SPROUTING BEANS

Beansprouts make a nutritious addition to a salad. Put the dried beans, seeds or grains (try mung beans, aduki beans or alfalfa seeds) in a large glass jar, filling it less than one-sixth full. Cover with muslin or cheesecloth secured by a rubber band, and fill the jar with cold water. Pour the water off and put the jar in a warm, dark spot. Rinse and drain daily. The sprouts will be ready to harvest in 3–6 days, and should be rinsed and drained before use.

COOK'S TIP

The best way to prepare an iceberg lettuce is to remove the core, then hold the head under the tap and run cold water into the cavity. This will gently force the leaves apart, making it easy to remove as many as you need. Discard any outer leaves that have been damaged.

Starters & Light Meals

Pear & Pecan Salad with Blue Cheese Dressing

INGREDIENTS

75g/3oz/¾ cup shelled pecan nuts,
roughly chopped
3 crisp eating pears
175g/6oz young spinach, leaves stripped
from stems
1 escarole or butterhead lettuce, separated
into leaves
1 radicchio lettuce, separated into leaves
salt and ground black pepper
warm crusty bread, to serve
BLUE CHEESE DRESSING
25g/1oz blue cheese, crumbled
45ml/3 tbsp natural yogurt
10ml/2 tsp lemon juice
15ml/1 tbsp olive oil
5ml/1 tsp snipped chives

SERVES 6

1 Make the dressing. Stir the cheese, yogurt and lemon juice together in a small bowl. Gradually add the olive oil, beating constantly. Stir in the chives and add salt and pepper to taste. Preheat the grill.

2 Spread out the pecans on a baking sheet. Toast under the grill until golden, taking care not to allow them to scorch. Cut the unpeeled pears into quarters. Carefully remove the cores, then cut each pear quarter into thin even slices.

3 Mix the salad leaves, and pears in a bowl. Add 30ml/2 tbsp of the dressing and toss lightly until the leaves are coated. Season. Divide among six plates,

scatter over the pecan nuts and serve with crusty bread. Offer the remaining dressing separately.

Lobster Salad

INGREDIENTS

1 or 2 medium cooked lobsters
675g / 1½lb new potatoes, scrubbed
4 oranges
200g / 7oz can young artichokes in brine,
drained and quartered
60ml / 4 tbsp extra virgin olive oil
½ frisée lettuce, separated into leaves
175g / 6oz lamb's lettuce
2 tomatoes, peeled, seeded and diced
1 small bunch tarragon, chervil or flat leaf parsley
ORANGE BUTTER DRESSING
30ml / 2 tbsp frozen concentrated
orange juice, thawed
75g / 3oz / 6 tbsp butter, diced
salt and cayenne pepper

SERVES 4

1 Twist off the legs and claws from the lobster(s), and separate the tail piece from the body section. Break the claws open with a hammer and remove the meat in one piece. Use scissors to cut away the thin underside of the tail shell. Gently pull out the meat in one piece. Cut into slices and set aside.

2 Place the potatoes in a large saucepan of salted water. Bring to the boil, lower the heat slightly and cook for 15–20 minutes or until just tender. Drain and leave to cool.

3 Placing each orange in turn on a board, slice off the top and bottom neatly, taking care to remove all the pith. Using the same knife, cut off the peel on the sides of the orange, following the contours of the fruit. Then, holding the fruit over a bowl to catch the juice, slice very carefully between the membranes to remove the segments. Put the orange segments to one side. Remove the skin from the potatoes and cut them in half. Toss the orange segments, potatoes and artichokes lightly with a little of the olive oil.

4 Make the dressing. Place the thawed orange juice in a heatproof bowl set over a pan of simmering water. Heat for 1 minute, then turn off the heat and whisk in the butter, a little at a time, until the dressing reaches a coating consistency. Add salt and a pinch of cayenne to taste. If necessary, thin the dressing with some of the fresh orange juice. Cover the dressing and keep it warm.

5 Toss the prepared salad leaves with some of the remaining olive oil in a bowl, then arrange them on four or six plates, depending on whether the salad is to be served as a starter or light meal. Following the illustration opposite, or a composition of your own, add the potatoes, artichokes, orange segments and lobster slices. Spoon the warm orange dressing over the top, add the diced tomato and garnish with the fresh herbs. Serve at room temperature.

Tabbouleh

INGREDIENTS

115g/ 4oz/ ⅔ cup bulgur wheat
225g/ 8oz tomatoes, peeled and seeded
1 small red onion, chopped
3 spring onions, chopped
2 fat garlic cloves, crushed
50g/ 2oz fresh parsley, finely chopped
60ml/ 4 tbsp chopped fresh mint
120ml/ 4fl oz/ ½ cup olive oil
75ml/ 5 tbsp lemon juice
salt and ground black pepper
black olives and mint leaves, to garnish

SERVES 6

1 Place the bulgur in a sieve and rinse under cold running water until the water runs clear. Place in a bowl, cover with fresh cold water and leave to soak for 1 hour. Line the sieve with a clean dish towel, pour in the bulgur and drain thoroughly. Gather up the sides of the dish towel and squeeze well to remove all the excess moisture. Carefully tip the bulgur into a mixing bowl.

2 Cut the tomatoes into small dice, then stir them into the bulgur wheat with the red onion, spring onions, garlic and parsley. Add the mint and mix well.

3 Whisk together the olive oil and lemon juice in a small bowl, and season. Pour this dressing over the salad. Toss gently so the dressing is absorbed. Taste, and add more salt, pepper and lemon juice if liked. Serve at room temperature, garnished with sliced black olives and whole mint leaves.

Minted Melon Salad

INGREDIENTS

1 ripe orange-fleshed melon
1 ripe green or white-fleshed melon
mint sprigs, to garnish
DRESSING
30ml/2 tbsp roughly chopped fresh mint
5ml/1 tsp caster sugar
30ml/2 tbsp raspberry vinegar
90ml/6 tbsp extra virgin olive oil
salt and ground black pepper

SERVES 6

1 Cut the melons in half, then scoop out and discard the seeds. Using a sharp knife, cut the melons into thin slices. Carefully remove the skins. Take six individual salad plates and arrange slices of the two varieties of melon decoratively on each one.

2 Make the dressing. Mix together the mint, sugar and raspberry vinegar in a small bowl. Gradually whisk in the oil, then add salt and pepper to taste. Alternatively, mix all the ingredients in a screw-top jar, close tightly and shake vigorously to combine.

3 Spoon the dressing over the melon slices. Serve lightly chilled and garnished with mint sprigs.

Aubergine & Red Pepper Pâté with Radicchio

INGREDIENTS

1 radicchio lettuce, separated into leaves
1 butterhead lettuce, separated into leaves
crispbreads, to serve
PATE
3 aubergines
2 red peppers
5 garlic cloves
7.5ml / 1½ tsp pink peppercorns in brine,
drained and crushed (optional)
30ml / 2 tbsp chopped fresh coriander

SERVES 6

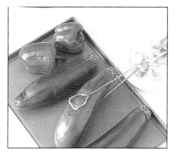

1 Make the pâté. Preheat the oven to 200°C/400°F/ Gas 6. Arrange the whole aubergines, peppers and the unpeeled garlic cloves on a baking sheet. Bake for 10 minutes, then remove the garlic cloves. Turn the vegetables over and bake for 20 minutes more. Peel the garlic and put into a food processor or blender.

2 Remove the charred red peppers from the oven. Place in a plastic bag, close tightly and leave to cool. Bake the aubergines for a further 10 minutes.

3 Remove the aubergines from the oven, split them in half and scoop the flesh into a sieve placed over a bowl. Press the flesh with a spoon to remove the bitter juices, then add to the garlic. Process until smooth, then scrape into a large bowl.

4 Remove the red peppers from the plastic bag and rub or peel off the skins and discard. Remove and discard the seeds, then chop the flesh finely. Stir the diced peppers into the aubergine and garlic mixture together with the pink peppercorns, if using, and the chopped fresh coriander.

5 Choose a few radicchio and butterhead lettuce leaves of similar size and arrange them in an attractive pattern around the edges of six individual salad plates. Place a few spoonfuls of the aubergine and red pepper pâté in the centre of each plate of salad. Serve at once, with crispbreads, if liked.

18

Melon & Parma Ham Salad

INGREDIENTS

1 large melon (cantaloupe, Galia or Charentais)
175g/6oz Parma or Serrano ham, thinly sliced
SALSA
225g/8oz strawberries, hulled
5ml/1 tsp caster sugar
30ml/2 tbsp groundnut or sunflower oil
15ml/1 tbsp orange juice
2.5ml/½ tsp finely grated orange rind
2.5ml/½ tsp finely grated fresh root ginger
salt and ground black pepper

SERVES 4

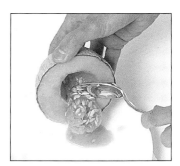

1 Cut the melon in half and then scoop out and discard the seeds. Using a sharp knife, cut the melon into thick slices. Carefully remove the skin. Place the slices on a large plate in a single layer, cover and chill in the fridge until ready to serve.

2 Make the salsa. Cut the strawberries into large dice. Place them in a bowl with the sugar and crush lightly to release the juices. Add the oil, orange juice, orange rind and ginger. Season with salt and a generous grinding of black pepper.

3 Arrange the melon on a serving plate and drape the ham over the top. Serve with strawberry salsa.

Smoked Trout & Horseradish Salad

INGREDIENTS

675g / 1½lb new potatoes, scrubbed
115g / 4oz mixed lettuce leaves
4 smoked trout fillets, skinned and flaked
4 slices of dark rye bread, cut into small fingers
4 cherry tomatoes, halved
salt and ground black pepper
DRESSING
60ml / 4 tbsp creamed horseradish
15ml / 1 tbsp white wine vinegar
60ml / 4 tbsp groundnut oil
10ml / 2 tsp caraway seeds

SERVES 4

1 Place the potatoes in a large pan of salted water. Bring to the boil, lower the heat slightly and cook for 15–20 minutes or until just tender. Drain and cool.

2 Make the dressing. Mix the horseradish and vinegar in a small bowl. Whisk in the oil. Stir in the caraway seeds. Alternatively, mix the ingredients in a screw-top jar, close tightly and shake to combine.

3 Put the prepared salad leaves in a bowl. Season with salt and pepper and toss with a little of the dressing. Cut the potatoes in half. Arrange the trout, potatoes, rye fingers and cherry tomatoes on the salad, drizzle over a little more dressing and serve. Offer the remaining dressing separately.

Main Course Salads

New Orleans Steak Salad

INGREDIENTS

4 sirloin or rump steaks, about 175g/6oz each
1 butterhead lettuce, separated into leaves
1 bunch watercress, trimmed
4 tomatoes, quartered
4 drained canned artichoke hearts, halved
175g/6oz button mushrooms, sliced
4 spring onions, sliced
4 large gherkins, sliced
a few green olives
salt and ground black pepper
FRENCH DRESSING
15ml/1 tbsp white wine vinegar
5ml/1 tsp Dijon mustard
pinch of caster sugar
90ml/6 tbsp extra virgin olive oil

SERVES 4

1 Preheat the grill. Season the steaks with black pepper. Place them on a rack over a grill pan and cook for 6–8 minutes, turning once, until they are medium rare. Cover the steaks with domed foil and leave in a warm place while you assemble the rest of the salad.

2 Make the dressing. Mix the vinegar, mustard and sugar in a small bowl, then whisk in the oil. Alternatively, mix all the ingredients in a screw-top jar, close tightly and shake to combine.

3 Put the prepared lettuce, watercress, tomatoes, artichoke hearts and mushrooms in a bowl. Add the dressing and toss together lightly. Divide the salad among four plates and arrange the spring onions, gherkins and olives on each. Slice each steak diagonally and arrange over the salads. Season with salt and pepper and serve at once.

Goat's Cheese Salad with Buckwheat, Fresh Figs & Walnuts

INGREDIENTS

175g/6oz/1½ cups couscous
30ml/2 tbsp toasted buckwheat
30ml/2 tbsp chopped fresh parsley
60ml/4 tbsp olive oil
45ml/3 tbsp walnut oil
115g/4oz rocket leaves
½ frisée lettuce, separated into leaves
175g/6oz crumbly white goat's cheese
50g/2oz/½ cup walnut pieces, toasted
4 ripe figs
salt and ground black pepper

SERVES 4

1 Mix the couscous and buckwheat together in a heatproof bowl. Pour over enough boiling water to cover and leave to soak for 15 minutes. Drain well in a sieve, then spread the mixture out on a metal tray and set aside to dry out a little more.

2 Tip the couscous mixture into a bowl. Add the chopped fresh parsley. Mix the olive oil and walnut oil together, add half the dressing to the couscous mixture and toss lightly. Season to taste with plenty of salt and ground black pepper

3 Place the prepared rocket and frisée leaves in a separate bowl, add the remaining oil mixture and toss to coat. Arrange the dressed salad leaves on four large plates, especially around the edges, and pile couscous mixture in the centre of each one.

4 Crumble or cube the goat's cheese and arrange it over the salads, then scatter with the toasted walnut pieces. Using a sharp knife, carefully cut each fig into four from the top almost to the base. Leave the quarters joined at the base so that they open out like the petals of a flower. Gently centre a fig on each salad and serve immediately.

24

Grilled Salmon & Spring Vegetable Salad

INGREDIENTS

350g/12oz small new potatoes, scrubbed
4 quail's eggs
115g/4oz baby courgettes, topped and tailed
115g/4oz young carrots, peeled
115g/4oz baby sweetcorn
115g/4oz sugar snap peas, trimmed
115g/4oz fine green beans, trimmed
115g/4oz patty pan squash (optional)
120ml/4fl oz French dressing
4 salmon fillets, about 150g/5oz each, skinned
115g/4oz sorrel or young spinach, leaves
stripped from stems
salt and ground black pepper

SERVES 4

1 Put the potatoes in a pan of salted water. Bring to the boil, lower the heat slightly and cook for 15–20 minutes or until just tender. Drain and keep warm.

2 Put the quail's eggs in a pan. Add boiling water to cover and simmer for 7–8 minutes. Cool under cold running water. Shell the eggs and cut them in half.

3 Peel the courgettes decoratively. Cook the carrots, sweetcorn, peas, beans, courgettes and squash (if using) in a pan of boiling water for about 2 minutes.

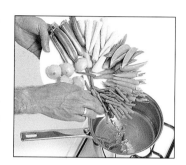

Drain well and put in a bowl. Add the potatoes. Toss with a little French dressing, season and allow to cool. Preheat the grill.

4 Put the salmon fillets on a rack over a grill pan, brush with a little of the dressing and grill them for 6 minutes, turning once. Meanwhile, put the sorrel or

spinach leaves in a stainless steel or enamel saucepan. Add 60ml/4 tbsp of the dressing, cover and soften over a gentle heat for 2 minutes. Strain the sorrel or spinach and cool to room temperature.

5 Arrange the salmon, spring vegetables and potatoes on four large plates. Place a spoonful of sorrel or spinach on each piece of salmon, top with a halved hard-boiled quail's egg and serve.

Wild Rice & Turkey Salad

INGREDIENTS

175g/6oz/1 cup wild rice
2 celery sticks, thinly sliced
3 spring onions, chopped
115g/4oz button mushrooms, quartered
450g/1lb cooked turkey breast, diced
5ml/1 tsp fresh thyme leaves
120ml/4fl oz French dressing, made with
walnut oil
2 dessert pears
25g/1oz/¼ cup walnut pieces, toasted
salt
4 thyme sprigs, to garnish

SERVES 4

1 Bring a large saucepan of lightly salted water to the boil. Add the wild rice, bring back to a gentle boil and cook for 40–50 minutes, or until the rice is tender but still firm and the grains have begun to split. Drain well. When cool, tip into a bowl.

2 Add the celery, spring onions, mushrooms, diced turkey and fresh thyme to the bowl. Pour over the French dressing and toss together gently to coat.

3 Cut the pears in half. Peel them and remove the cores, then thinly slice the halves lengthways without cutting through the stalk end. Spread the slices out like a fan.

4 Spoon the salad on to four plates, leaving a space on each for a fanned pear. Add the pears and walnuts and garnish with the thyme. Serve at once.

Gruyère, Chicken & Tongue Salad

INGREDIENTS

2 boned and skinned chicken breasts, cooked
225g/8oz cooked ox tongue or ham, sliced
5mm/¼in thick
225g/8oz Gruyère cheese
1 lollo rosso lettuce, separated into leaves
1 butterhead lettuce, separated into leaves
1 bunch watercress, trimmed
3 celery sticks, thinly sliced
2 green-skinned eating apples
60ml/4 tbsp sesame seeds, toasted
salt and ground black pepper
grated nutmeg
DRESSING
45ml/3 tbsp lemon juice
10ml/2 tsp chopped fresh mint
3 drops of Tabasco sauce
75ml/5 tbsp groundnut or sunflower oil
5ml/1 tsp sesame oil

SERVES 4

1 Make the dressing. Mix the lemon juice, mint and Tabasco in a small bowl. Gradually whisk in the oils. Alternatively, mix all the ingredients in a screw-top jar, close tightly and shake to combine.

2 Slice the chicken, tongue or ham and cheese into fine strips. Place in a bowl, moisten with a little of the dressing and set aside.

3 Put the prepared lettuce leaves, watercress and celery in a separate bowl and gently mix together. Quarter and core the apples, then slice them directly into the bowl. Add the remaining dressing and toss lightly together until well coated.

4 Place the salad on four plates. Pile the meat and cheese strips in the centre. Scatter with the sesame seeds, season with salt, pepper and nutmeg and serve.

29

Avocado, Crab & Coriander Salad

INGREDIENTS

675g/1½ lb small new potatoes, scrubbed
1 mint sprig
*900g/2lb boiled crab or 275g/10oz frozen
crabmeat, thawed*
*1 butterhead or escarole lettuce, separated
into leaves*
175g/6oz lamb's lettuce or young spinach leaves
175g/6oz cherry tomatoes
1 large ripe avocado
salt and ground black pepper
grated nutmeg
DRESSING
15ml/1 tbsp freshly squeezed lime juice
45ml/3 tbsp chopped fresh coriander
2.5ml/½ tsp caster sugar
75ml/5 tbsp olive oil

SERVES 4

1 Place the potatoes in a large saucepan of salted water. Add the mint. Bring to the boil, lower the heat slightly and cook for 15–20 minutes or until just tender. Drain, cover and keep warm until needed.

2 Lay the crab on its back and twist off the legs and claws where they join the body. Crack them open with the back of a chopping knife or lobster cracker and pick out the white meat with a skewer.

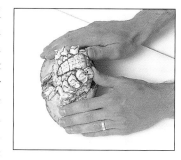

3 Hold the shell firmly and push the body section upwards, easing it out with your thumbs. Remove the flesh from inside the shell, then discard the grey feather-like gills. Crack the body section open and remove the white and dark flesh with a skewer.

4 Make the dressing. Mix the lime juice, coriander and sugar in a small bowl. Gradually whisk in the oil. Alternatively, mix all the ingredients in a screw-top jar, close tightly and shake to combine. Toss the prepared salad leaves with a little of the dressing.

5 Place the salad on four large plates and distribute the cherry tomatoes among them. Cut the avocado in half and remove the stone and the skin. Slice thinly and arrange on the salads. Top the salads with the crab and distribute the warm new potatoes among them. Drizzle with the dressing, season with salt, pepper and nutmeg and serve.

Warm Salads

Wild Mushroom Salad with Parma Ham

INGREDIENTS

175g/6oz Parma ham, thickly sliced
40g/1½ oz/3 tbsp butter
450g/1lb wild and cultivated mushrooms
(chanterelles, field blewits, oyster mushrooms,
champignons de Paris), sliced
½ oakleaf lettuce, separated into leaves
½ frisée lettuce, separated into leaves
15ml/1 tbsp walnut oil
60ml/4 tbsp brandy
HERB PANCAKES
45ml/3 tbsp plain flour
75ml/5 tbsp milk
1 egg plus 1 egg yolk
60ml/4 tbsp freshly grated Parmesan cheese
45ml/3 tbsp chopped mixed fresh herbs
salt and ground black pepper

SERVES 4

1 Make the pancakes. Mix the flour and milk in a measuring jug. Beat in the egg, egg yolk, Parmesan and herbs. Add salt and pepper to taste. Place a lightly greased frying pan over a steady heat. Pour in enough mixture to coat the bottom of the pan.

2 When the batter has set, flip the pancake over and cook the other side, then turn out. Cook more pancakes in the same way. When the pancakes are cool, roll them up together and slice into ribbons.

3 Cut the ham into strips to match the pancake ribbons and toss them lightly together in a bowl. Heat the butter in the clean frying pan. Add the mushrooms and cook for 6–8 minutes.

4 Meanwhile dress the prepared salad leaves with walnut oil. Divide them among four large plates and arrange the ham and pancake ribbons in the centre of each one. Add the brandy to the mushrooms and ignite it. As soon as the flames die down, spoon the mushrooms over the salads. Season with salt and pepper, and serve.

Warm Duck Salad with Orange & Coriander

INGREDIENTS

1 small orange
2 boned duck breasts
150ml/¼ pint/⅔ cup dry white wine
5ml/1 tsp ground coriander
2.5ml/½ tsp ground cumin
30ml/2 tbsp caster sugar
juice of ½ lime or small lemon
½ escarole lettuce, separated into leaves
½ frisée lettuce, separated into leaves
30ml/2 tbsp sunflower oil
salt and cayenne pepper
4 coriander sprigs, to garnish
GARLIC CROUTONS
1 garlic clove
45ml/3 tbsp olive oil
75g/3oz thickly sliced day-old bread,
cut into short fingers

SERVES 4

1 Cut the orange in half, then into thick slices. Discard any pips and place the slices in a small saucepan. Add water to cover, heat to simmering and cook for 5 minutes. Drain and set aside.

2 Prick the skin on the duck breasts, then rub the skin with salt. Heat a heavy-based frying pan, add the duck breasts and cook for 20 minutes, turning once, until they are medium-rare.

3 Transfer the duck breasts to a heated plate, cover and keep hot. Pour off the fat from the pan, leaving the sediment behind.

4 Add the wine, spices and sugar to the frying pan and stir over the heat, taking care to incorporate the sediment. Add the orange slices. Boil quickly until the sauce coats the oranges, then sharpen with the lime or lemon juice. Add salt and cayenne to taste and keep warm over a low heat.

5 Make the croûtons in a second frying pan. Peel and bruise the garlic clove. Heat the olive oil with the garlic and when the garlic turns a deep golden brown, remove it with a slotted spoon. Add the bread fingers to the pan and fry until golden brown. Remove and drain on kitchen paper.

6 Sprinkle the prepared lettuce leaves with the sunflower oil and arrange on four large plates. Cut the duck breasts into thick slices diagonally. Using  the composition illustrated opposite, or one of your own, add the duck and glazed orange slices to the plates. Scatter with the croûtons, garnish each salad with a coriander sprig and serve.

Spinach & Bacon Salad

INGREDIENTS

*450g / 1lb young spinach, leaves stripped
from stems
60ml / 4 tbsp red wine vinegar
60ml / 4 tbsp water
20ml / 4 tsp caster sugar
5ml / 1 tsp dry mustard
25ml / 1½ tbsp sunflower oil
225g / 8oz rindless streaky bacon rashers
8 spring onions, thinly sliced
6 radishes, thinly sliced
2 hard-boiled eggs, coarsely grated
salt and ground black pepper*

SERVES 6

1 Put the prepared spinach leaves in a large salad bowl. Mix the vinegar, water, sugar and dry mustard in a separate bowl. Add a pinch of salt and a grinding of black pepper.

2 Heat the oil in a frying pan, add the bacon rashers and fry until very crisp and brown. Remove them with tongs and drain them well on kitchen paper.

3 Add the vinegar mixture to the bacon fat remaining in the pan. Bring to the boil, stirring constantly to incorporate any sediment on the base of the pan. Immediately pour the hot dressing over the spinach salad. Toss quickly to coat the leaves well.

4 Chop the bacon roughly and add it to the spinach. Add the spring onions and radishes and mix gently. Scatter the grated hard-boiled egg over the salad, season to taste and serve at once.

Green Lentil & Cabbage Salad

INGREDIENTS

225g/8oz/1 cup Puy or green lentils, soaked
in cold water to cover for 2 hours
600ml/1 pint/2½ cups water
3 garlic cloves
1 bay leaf
1 small onion, peeled and studded with 2 cloves
15ml/1 tbsp olive oil
1 red onion, thinly sliced
15ml/1 tbsp thyme leaves
350g/12oz cabbage, finely shredded
finely grated rind and juice of 1 lemon
15ml/1 tbsp raspberry or red wine vinegar
salt and ground black pepper

SERVES 4–6

1 Drain the lentils and place them in a large saucepan. Pour over the water. Peel one garlic clove, leaving it whole, and add it to the saucepan with the bay leaf and studded onion. Bring to the boil and cook over a high heat for 10 minutes. Lower the heat, cover and cook for 25–35 minutes or until the lentils are tender. Remove the bay leaf and onion.

2 Meanwhile gently heat the oil in a large pan. Peel and crush the remaining garlic cloves and add them to the pan with the red onion and thyme. Cook for 10 minutes or until the onion is soft.

3 Add the cabbage, raise the heat and cook for 3–5 minutes, until just cooked but still crunchy. Drain the lentils if necessary and add them to the pan with the lemon rind and juice, and the vinegar.

4 Season the warm salad generously with salt and pepper, spoon into a bowl and serve at once with warm crusty French bread, if liked.

Mussel & Lentil Salad

INGREDIENTS

60ml/4 tbsp olive oil
1 onion, finely chopped
350g/12oz/1½ cups Puy or green lentils,
soaked in cold water to cover for 2 hours
900ml/1½ pints/3¾ cups vegetable stock
2 large carrots, cut into matchsticks
4 celery sticks, cut into matchsticks
900g/2lb young spinach, leaves stripped
from stems
1 garlic clove, halved
2kg/4½lb live mussels, scrubbed and bearded
75ml/5 tbsp white wine
generous pinch of saffron strands
2.5ml/½ tsp mild curry paste
30ml/2 tbsp double cream
salt and cayenne pepper

SERVES 4

1 Heat 45ml/3 tbsp of the oil in a saucepan and cook the onion on a low heat for 10 minutes. Add the drained lentils and stock to the pan. Bring to the boil and cook for 10 minutes. Lower the heat, cover and cook for 25–35 minutes until tender.

2 Meanwhile bring a small pan of water to the boil. Cook the carrot and celery matchsticks for about 3 minutes. Drain, cool, put in a bowl and moisten with some of the remaining oil.

3 Rinse the spinach leaves and place in a clean pan. Cover tightly, steam for 30 seconds, then refresh under cold water. Drain well, pressing the leaves gently against the sides of the colander or sieve to extract the excess liquid. Rub the cut clove of garlic thoroughly around the inside of a bowl, tip in the spinach and toss with the remaining oil.

4 Discard any mussels which do not close when tapped. Place the rest in a large saucepan. Add the wine, cover and cook over a high heat for 5–8 minutes, shaking the pan frequently, until the mussels have opened. Discard any that remain closed. Drain, reserving the cooking liquid. When cool, remove all but 4 of the mussels from their shells.

5 Strain the mussel liquid through a fine sieve into a deep frying pan. Stir in the saffron strands and leave to soak for 5 minutes, then stir in the curry paste. Cook over a high heat until most of the liquid has evaporated. Remove from the heat, stir in the cream and add the shelled mussels, with salt and cayenne to taste. Toss to coat.

6 Drain the lentils if necessary and spoon them into the centre of four large plates. Surround each mound of lentils with five tiny heaps of spinach. Arrange a few carrot and celery matchsticks on top of each spinach portion. Spoon the mussels and sauce over the lentils. Garnish each plate with an opened mussel in the shell and serve warm.

Side Salads

Lettuce & Herb Salad

INGREDIENTS

½ cucumber
mixed salad leaves
1 bunch watercress, trimmed
1 head chicory, sliced
45ml/3 tbsp chopped mixed fresh herbs
(parsley, thyme, mint, tarragon and chives)
DRESSING
15ml/1 tbsp wine vinegar
5ml/1 tsp prepared mustard
75ml/5 tbsp olive oil
salt and ground black pepper

SERVES 4

1 Make the dressing. Put the wine vinegar and mustard in a small bowl and mix together. Whisk in the olive oil gradually and then add salt and pepper to taste. Alternatively, mix all the ingredients in a screw-top jar, close tightly and shake to combine.

2 Peel the cucumber, if liked, then halve it lengthways and scoop out the seeds. Thinly slice the flesh. Tear the prepared mixed salad leaves into bite-size pieces.

3 Mix together the cucumber, salad leaves, watercress, chicory and fresh herbs in a large bowl. Add the dressing and toss to coat. Serve the salad at once.

Apple & Date Coleslaw

INGREDIENTS

1 pear
1 red-skinned eating apple
225g/8oz red or white cabbage, or a mixture
3 carrots
200g/7oz can green flageolet beans, drained
50g/2oz/⅓ cup chopped dates
DRESSING
2.5ml/½ tsp dry English mustard
10ml/2 tsp clear honey
30ml/2 tbsp orange juice
5ml/1 tsp white wine vinegar
2.5ml/½ tsp paprika
salt and ground black pepper

SERVES 4–6

1 Make the dressing. In a small bowl, mix the mustard and honey until smooth. Add the orange juice, vinegar, paprika, salt and pepper to taste. Mix well.

2 Cut the pear and apple into quarters, leaving the skin on. Remove the cores and slice the fruit thinly. Place in a bowl and toss with a little of the dressing.

3 Cut away the core from the cabbage. Shred the cabbage leaves very finely, discarding any other tough portions. Cut the carrots into very thin

strips, about 5cm/2in long. Add the cabbage, carrots, flageolets and dates to the bowl. Mix well.

4 Pour over all the remaining dressing and toss thoroughly to coat. Cover the coleslaw and put in the fridge to chill for about 30 minutes before serving.

COOK'S TIP

Sultanas can be used instead of dates, if preferred. To plump them up, leave to marinate in the dressing for 15 minutes. Add the dressing and sultanas to the coleslaw and mix well.

Tomato & Feta Cheese Salad

INGREDIENTS

900g/2lb ripe tomatoes
200g/7oz feta cheese
120ml/4fl oz/½ cup extra virgin olive oil
12 black olives
ground black pepper
4 basil sprigs, to garnish (optional)

SERVES 4

1 Using a small, pointed knife cut around and then remove the tough cores from the tomatoes. Cut the tomatoes in thick slices and arrange in a shallow dish.

2 Crumble the feta cheese over the sliced tomatoes. Drizzle over the oil, add the olives and a grinding of black pepper. Garnish with the basil, if liked.

COOK'S TIP

It is traditional to use only olive oil when dressing tomato salads, but a dash of balsamic vinegar may be added to the oil if the tomatoes are particularly sweet, or if this is more to your taste.

Marinated Cucumber Salad

INGREDIENTS

2 cucumbers
15ml / 1 tbsp salt
90g / 3½oz / scant ½ cup sugar
175ml / 6fl oz / ¾ cup dry cider
15ml / 1 tbsp cider vinegar
45ml / 3 tbsp chopped fresh dill
ground black pepper

SERVES 4–6

45

1 Slice the cucumbers thinly and spread them in a colander, sprinkling salt between each layer. Set the colander over a bowl and leave to drain for 1 hour.

2 Meanwhile, mix the sugar, dry cider and cider vinegar in a saucepan. Heat gently, stirring continuously until the sugar has dissolved. Leave to become cold.

3 Rinse all the cucumber slices very thoroughly under cold running water to remove the excess salt, then pat dry on kitchen paper and place in a 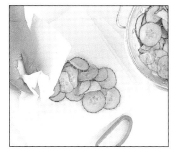 bowl. Pour over the cold cider mixture, cover and leave to marinate for 2 hours.

4 Drain the cucumber and sprinkle with the fresh dill and black pepper to taste. Transfer to a serving dish. Mix well, cover and chill until ready to serve.

Coronation Salad

INGREDIENTS

450g/ 1lb new potatoes, scrubbed
45ml/ 3 tbsp French dressing
3 spring onions, chopped
6 hard-boiled eggs, halved
1 frisée lettuce, separated into leaves
¼ cucumber, sliced, then cut into
very fine matchsticks
6 large radishes, sliced
salad cress
salt and ground black pepper
CURRY DRESSING
30ml/ 2 tbsp olive oil
1 small onion, finely chopped
15ml/ 1 tbsp mild curry powder or korma
spice mix
10ml/ 2 tsp tomato purée
30ml/ 2 tbsp lemon juice
30ml/ 2 tbsp sherry
300ml/ ½ pint/ 1¼ cups mayonnaise
150ml/ ¼ pint/ ⅔ cup natural yogurt

SERVES 6

1 Place the potatoes in a large saucepan of salted water. Bring to the boil, lower the heat slightly and cook for 15–20 minutes or until just tender. Drain the potatoes and tip them into a bowl. Add the French dressing and toss gently together until well coated. Set aside to cool.

2 Make the curry dressing. Heat the oil in a saucepan. Add the onion and fry for 5 minutes. Stir in the curry powder or spice mix and fry for a further 1 minute, then remove from the heat and add all the remaining dressing ingredients. Mix well.

3 Add the curry dressing, spring onions and salt and pepper, to taste, to the potatoes. Add the hard-boiled eggs and mix lightly, taking care not to break them up. Cover and chill until ready to serve.

4 Line a serving platter with the prepared lettuce leaves and pile the salad in the centre. Arrange the cucumber, radishes and snipped salad cress on top. Serve at once.

46

Pasta & Beetroot Salad

INGREDIENTS

2 uncooked beetroots, scrubbed
225g/8oz/2 cups dried pasta shells or twists
45ml/3 tbsp French dressing
2 celery sticks, thinly sliced
3 spring onions, sliced
75g/3oz/¾ cup walnuts or hazelnuts,
roughly chopped
1 eating apple
1 frisée lettuce, separated into leaves
3 hard-boiled eggs, chopped
2 avocados
salt and ground black pepper
snipped salad cress, to garnish
HORSERADISH DRESSING
60ml/4 tbsp mayonnaise
45ml/3 tbsp natural yogurt or fromage frais
30ml/2 tbsp milk
10ml/2 tsp creamed horseradish

SERVES 8

1 Put the beetroots in a large pan of salted water. Bring to the boil, lower the heat slightly and cook for 45–55 minutes or until just tender. Drain, rub off the skins and leave to cool. Once cold, cut the beetroots into neat dice.

2 Make the horseradish dressing by mixing all the ingredients in a bowl.

3 Bring a large saucepan of lightly salted water to the boil. Add the pasta and cook for 10–12 minutes, until *al dente*. Drain, tip into a bowl and toss with the French dressing. Season to taste.

4 Add the beetroots, celery, spring onions and nuts to the pasta. Core and thinly slice the apple and add it to the pasta mixture. Spoon the horseradish dressing over the top and mix well. Cover and chill.

5 Line a salad bowl with the prepared lettuce leaves. Pile the salad into the centre and scatter over the chopped egg. Peel, stone and slice the avocados and arrange on top. Garnish with the salad cress.

47

Leeks with Parsley, Egg & Walnut Dressing

INGREDIENTS

675g / 1½lb young leeks, trimmed
1 hard-boiled egg
sprig of parsley, to garnish
DRESSING
25g / 1oz fresh parsley
30ml / 2 tbsp olive oil
juice of ½ lemon
50g / 2oz / ½ cup walnut pieces, toasted
90ml / 6 tbsp water
5ml / 1 tsp caster sugar
salt and ground black pepper

SERVES 4

1 Cut the leeks into 10cm/4in lengths. Rinse very well in cold water to flush out any grit or soil. Bring a saucepan of lightly salted water to the boil. Add the leeks to the saucepan and cook for 8 minutes. Drain, refresh under cold running water and drain again.

2 Make the dressing. Chop the parsley finely in a food processor or blender. Add the olive oil, lemon juice and walnuts and process until smooth. Mix in enough of the water to give a coating consistency, then add the sugar, with salt and pepper to taste.

3 Arrange the leeks on a serving platter. Spoon the sauce over. Finely grate the hard-boiled egg over the sauce and serve garnished with a sprig of parsley.

COOK'S TIP
This recipe can also be made using fresh seasonal vegetables, such as green asparagus tips or baby courgettes, in place of the leeks. Cook only until just tender.

48

Green Salad with Orange & Avocado

INGREDIENTS

2 seedless oranges
45ml/3 tbsp lemon juice
5ml/1 tsp Dijon mustard
pinch of caster sugar
90ml/6 tbsp olive oil
15ml/1 tbsp walnut oil
1 round lettuce, separated into leaves
1 small bunch watercress, trimmed
a few frisée lettuce leaves
1 small bunch rocket, trimmed
1 red onion, thinly sliced in rings
1 avocado
50g/2oz/½ cup walnut pieces, toasted
salt and ground black pepper

SERVES 4

1 Grate the rind from 1 orange and set it aside. Placing each orange in turn on a board, slice off the top and bottom neatly, taking care to remove all the pith. Using the same knife, cut off the peel on the sides of the orange, following the contours of the fruit. Then, holding the fruit over a bowl to catch the juice, slice carefully between the membranes to remove the segments.

2 Add the grated orange rind, lemon juice, mustard and sugar to 30ml/2 tbsp of the orange juice. Gradually whisk in the oils, then add salt and pepper to taste. Alternatively, mix all the ingredients in a screw-top jar, close tightly and shake to combine.

3 Place the prepared salad leaves in a bowl with the onion rings and orange segments. Cut the avocado in half, remove the stone and peel off the skin. Cut the flesh into cubes and add them to the bowl.

4 Pour over the orange dressing, toss gently to coat, scatter the walnuts on top and serve.

Watercress & Potato Salad

INGREDIENTS

450g / 1lb small new potatoes, scrubbed
1 bunch watercress, trimmed
200g / 7oz cherry tomatoes, halved
30ml / 2 tbsp pumpkin seeds
DRESSING
45ml / 3 tbsp fromage frais
15ml / 1 tbsp cider vinegar
5ml / 1 tsp soft light brown sugar
salt and paprika

SERVES 4

1 Put the potatoes in a large saucepan of salted water. Bring to the boil, lower the heat slightly and cook for 15–20 minutes or until just tender. Drain and cool.

2 Meanwhile make the dressing. Put the fromage frais, cider vinegar, sugar, salt and paprika to taste, into a small bowl. Using a small hand whisk, beat together until well combined. Alternatively, mix all the dressing ingredients in a screw-top jar, close tightly and shake vigorously to combine.

3 Mix the potatoes, watercress, tomatoes and pumpkin seeds in a salad bowl. Pour over the dressing and serve at once.

COOK'S TIP

For a variation on this salad try using a mixture of watercress and baby spinach or rocket leaves and replace the pumpkin seeds with sunflower seeds or toasted pine nuts.

Classic Salads

Chef's Salad

INGREDIENTS

450g/1lb small new potatoes, scrubbed
1 iceberg or round lettuce, or 1 head chicory,
separated into leaves
2 carrots, coarsely grated
½ small fennel bulb or 2 celery sticks,
finely sliced
50g/2oz small button mushrooms, sliced
¼ cucumber, chopped
1 small green or red pepper, seeded, cut in half
and sliced
60ml/4 tbsp cooked peas or mange-touts
200g/7oz/1 cup cooked pulses (lentils,
red kidney beans, butter beans)
2-3 hard-boiled eggs, quartered
salt and ground black pepper
salad cress, to garnish
DRESSING
60ml/4 tbsp mayonnaise
45ml/3 tbsp natural yogurt
30ml/2 tbsp milk
30ml/2 tbsp snipped chives

SERVES 6

1 Place the potatoes in a large saucepan of salted water. Bring to the boil, lower the heat slightly and cook for 15–20 minutes or until just tender. Drain and leave to cool.

2 Make the dressing. Put all the dressing ingredients in a small bowl and mix together well with a fork or hand whisk. Add salt and pepper to taste.

3 Line a large serving platter with the prepared lettuce or chicory leaves. Mix the potatoes with all the other vegetables and pulses in a large bowl. Add salt and pepper to taste. Pour the dressing over the salad and toss together thoroughly.

4 Spoon the potato mixture on to the bed of lettuce or chicory leaves, top with the eggs and garnish with snipped cress. Serve lightly chilled.

53

Salade Niçoise

INGREDIENTS

675g/1½lb potatoes, peeled
225g/8oz green beans, topped and tailed
225g/8oz small plum tomatoes, quartered,
or cherry tomatoes
120ml/4fl oz French dressing
1 cos lettuce, separated into leaves
400g/14oz can tuna in oil,
drained and broken into large flakes
3 hard-boiled eggs, quartered
½ x 50g/2oz can anchovy fillets, drained
30ml/2 tbsp rinsed capers
12 black olives
salt and ground black pepper

SERVES 4

1 Place the potatoes in a large saucepan of salted water. Bring to the boil, lower the heat slightly and cook for 15–20 minutes. Drain, cool under cold running water and drain again. Slice thickly.

2 Cook the beans in a second pan of boiling water for 6 minutes. Drain, refresh under cold running water and drain again.

3 Mix together the potato slices, beans and plum or cherry tomatoes in a bowl. Add half of the French dressing and toss gently together until well coated.

4 Chop or tear the prepared lettuce leaves roughly and place them in a large salad bowl. Pour the rest of the French dressing over the salad leaves and toss together very lightly. Add the potato slices, beans and tomatoes to the dressed leaves and divide among individual serving plates.

5 Distribute the flaked tuna over the salads with the hard-boiled egg quarters, anchovy fillets, capers and olives, pitted if liked. Season to taste and serve the salads at once.

Caesar Salad

INGREDIENTS

2 thick slices of bread, crusts removed
45ml/3 tbsp sunflower oil
2 whole peeled garlic cloves
1 cos lettuce, separated into leaves
50g/2oz/½ cup freshly grated Parmesan cheese
DRESSING
2 eggs
10ml/2 tsp Dijon mustard
10ml/2 tsp Worcestershire sauce
30ml/2 tbsp lemon juice
45ml/3 tbsp extra virgin olive oil

SERVES 4

1 Preheat the oven to 190°C/375°F/Gas 5. Cut the bread into cubes. Heat the oil gently in a saucepan. Add one of the garlic cloves and cook until golden. Remove the garlic then add the bread cubes and toss to coat in the flavoured oil.

2 Spread out the garlic-flavoured bread cubes on a baking sheet. Bake in the oven for 10–12 minutes until golden and crisp. Leave to cool.

3 Cut the remaining garlic clove in half. Rub the cut sides around the inside of a large salad bowl. Tear the prepared lettuce leaves into pieces and toss them into the bowl, sprinkling Parmesan cheese between the layers. Cover the salad and set aside.

4 Make the dressing. Bring a small saucepan of water to the boil. Add the eggs and cook for 1 minute only. Remove with a slotted spoon. Crack the eggs open into a jug or bowl. The whites should be milky and the yolks raw.

5 Add the remaining dressing ingredients to the eggs and whisk well. To serve, pour the dressing over the leaves, toss well and top with the croûtons.

COOK'S TIP

As the eggs for the dressing are barely cooked they must be perfectly fresh and bought from a reputable supplier, and the dressing should be made only just before serving.

Waldorf Ham Salad

INGREDIENTS

3 eating apples
15ml / 1 tbsp lemon juice
2 slices of cooked ham, about 175g / 6oz each
3 celery sticks
150ml / ¼ pint / ⅔ cup mayonnaise
½ bunch watercress, trimmed
1 escarole lettuce, separated into leaves
1 small radicchio lettuce, separated into leaves
45ml / 3 tbsp walnut oil or olive oil
50g / 2oz / ½ cup walnut pieces, toasted
salt and ground black pepper

SERVES 4

1 Quarter, peel and core the apples. Cut them into fine shreds, put in a bowl and toss with the lemon juice to prevent them turning brown.

2 Cut the ham and celery into 5cm / 2in strips and add to the apples. Spoon the mayonnaise over the apple, ham and celery mixture and toss to coat.

3 Slice the prepared escarole and radicchio lettuce leaves into fine shreds, put in a bowl and toss with the oil. Either set aside the watercress sprigs for garnishing or toss them with the lettuce now. Divide the dressed leaves among four plates.

4 Pile the mayonnaise mixture in the centre of each bed of leaves. Season with salt and pepper. Scatter the toasted walnuts on top and serve the salads at once, garnished with the watercress sprigs, if these have not yet been used.

58

Russian Salad

INGREDIENTS

115g/4oz large button mushrooms
350g/12oz cooked prawns, peeled and deveined
1 large gherkin, chopped, or 30ml/2 tbsp
rinsed capers
120ml/4fl oz/½ cup mayonnaise
15ml/1 tbsp lemon juice
115g/4oz small new potatoes, scrubbed
115g/4oz young carrots
115g/4oz baby sweetcorn
115g/4oz baby turnips, trimmed
115g/4oz broad beans
15ml/1 tbsp olive oil
4 hard-boiled eggs
½ x 50g/2oz can anchovy fillets, drained
and cut into fine strips, to garnish
salt and ground black pepper
paprika

SERVES 4

1 Slice the mushrooms thinly and cut into matchsticks. Put in a bowl with the prawns and gherkin or capers. Mix the mayonnaise and lemon juice in a small bowl and fold half into the mushroom mixture. Add salt and pepper to taste and mix gently.

2 Place the potatoes in a large saucepan of salted water. Bring to the boil, lower the heat slightly and cook for 15–20 minutes or until just tender.

3 Cook the carrots, sweetcorn and turnips in a separate pan of salted, boiling water for 6 minutes.

4 Bring another pan of salted water to the boil. Add the broad beans and cook for 3 minutes. Drain and refresh under cold water. Pinch each bean between your fingers to pop off the skins, revealing a tender green bean. Discard the skins.

5 Drain the potatoes and other vegetables, cool them under cold running water and drain well. Tip into a bowl, moisten with olive oil, then divide among four salad bowls. Spoon on the skinned broad beans and dressed prawns. Place a hard-boiled egg in the centre of each salad, garnish with strips of anchovy and sprinkle with paprika.

Gado Gado

INGREDIENTS

2 potatoes, peeled
175g/6oz green beans, trimmed
1 cos lettuce, washed and trimmed
3 hard-boiled eggs, quartered
½ cucumber, peeled and cut into fingers
350g/12oz large cooked prawns
115g/4oz beansprouts
150g/5oz mooli, peeled and grated
1 small bunch fresh coriander
175g/6oz bean curd, cut into large dice
4 tomatoes, cut into wedges
SPICY PEANUT SAUCE
2 shallots or 1 small onion, chopped
150g/5oz/½ cup smooth peanut butter
juice of ½ lemon
1 garlic clove, crushed
2 small red chillies, seeded and finely chopped
30ml/2 tbsp South-east Asian fish sauce (optional)
150ml/¼ pint/⅔ cup coconut milk, canned or fresh
15ml/1 tbsp caster sugar

SERVES 4

1 Make the peanut sauce. Put all the sauce ingredients into a food processor or blender and process until smooth. Scrape into a bowl and set aside.

2 Place the potatoes in a large saucepan of salted water. Bring to the boil, lower the heat slightly and cook for about 20 minutes or until just tender. Cook the beans in a separate pan of boiling water for 6 minutes. Drain the vegetables, refresh under cold running water and drain again. Leave to cool.

3 Use the outer leaves of the prepared cos lettuce to line a large platter. Pile the remaining leaves to one side of the platter. Slice the potatoes. Arrange the potatoes, beans, hard-boiled eggs, cucumber, prawns, beansprouts, mooli, coriander, bean curd and tomatoes in separate piles on the platter, leaving a space to accommodate the bowl of sauce.

4 Serve the salad lightly chilled with the peanut sauce in place. Guests make their own salad parcels, wrapping the fillings of their choice in lettuce leaves and dipping them in the spicy peanut sauce.

Prawn Salad with Curry Dressing

INGREDIENTS

1 ripe tomato
½ iceberg lettuce, shredded
1 small bunch fresh coriander, finely chopped
1 small onion, finely chopped
15ml/1 tbsp lemon juice
450g/1lb cooked prawns, peeled and deveined
1 eating apple
salt
DRESSING
75ml/5 tbsp mayonnaise
5ml/1 tsp mild curry paste
15ml/1 tbsp tomato ketchup
30ml/2 tbsp water
GARNISH
8 cooked prawns, in the shell
8 lemon wedges
4 fresh coriander sprigs

SERVES 4

1 Plunge the tomato into a saucepan of boiling water for 1 minute, then transfer it to a bowl of cold water. Slip off the skin, remove the core and seeds and cut the flesh into large dice.

2 Mix the lettuce, coriander, tomato and onion in a bowl. Moisten with the lemon juice and add salt to taste. Divide the mixture among four salad plates or bowls.

3 Make the dressing. Mix the mayonnaise, with the mild curry paste and ketchup in a small bowl. Stir in the water and add salt to taste. Mix with the peeled prawns and stir to combine. Quarter and core the apple and coarsely grate it into the mixture.

4 Pile a quarter of the prawn mixture on to each plate of salad, then garnish each with a couple of whole prawns, lemon wedges and finally a sprig of fresh coriander.

Index